DRUGS & CONSEQUENCES™

THE TRUTH ABOUT

PCP

CHRISTINE POOLOS

ROSEN
PUBLISHING®

New York

Published in 2014 by The Rosen Publishing Group, Inc.
29 East 21st Street, New York, NY 10010

Copyright © 2014 by The Rosen Publishing Group, Inc.

First Edition

Library of Congress Cataloging-in-Publication Data

Poolos, Christine.
The truth about PCP/Christine Poolos.—First edition.
    pages cm.—(Drugs & consequences)
Audience: Grades 7–12.
Includes bibliographical references and index.
ISBN 978-1-4777-1899-5 (library binding)
1. Phencyclidine—Juvenile literature. 2. Phencyclidine—United States—Juvenile literature. 3. Phencyclidine abuse—United States—Juvenile literature. I. Title.
HV5822.P45P66 2014
362.29'4—dc23

                                                                2013019268

Manufactured in the United States of America

CPSIA Compliance Information: Batch #W14YA: For further information, contact Rosen Publishing, New York, New York, at 1-800-237-9932.

CONTENTS

There is a new drug, or rather a new old drug, that has been making the rounds in a big city near you. Phencyclidine, better known as PCP, has come back more than a decade after it went away. Statistically, PCP doesn't seem to be much of an issue. The number of Americans using the drug isn't even close to the number of users of almost any other illegal drug. In fact, many people—especially those who remember the drug as "angel dust" from the 1960s and 1970s—don't even know that PCP still exists. Why should we worry about a substance that, statistically speaking, doesn't seem to be a scourge on society? What is PCP and what is the harm in it?

PCP is an illegal hallucinogen that can cause psychotic episodes. It is manufactured by street gangs and distributed around the country. It is not approved by the Food and Drug Administration (FDA), and users can't be sure of exactly what they're getting when they buy it. Use of the drug can be fairly harmless, but it can also result in extreme violence, danger, and severe mental problems.

Now sold in many forms, including a convenient and cheap cigarette, PCP is a drug whose use is on the increase. The U.S. Department of

PCP's low price makes it a diabolically tempting drug for teens looking for a quick and cheap high. Far from delivering a high, however, PCP use can often result in harrowing, violent, and even deadly "trips."

Justice reported that about six million U.S. residents aged twelve and older have used PCP at least once. And many of its users are teens. A survey of high school seniors found that more than 3 percent had used PCP at least once, while more than 1 percent had used it in the past year. Those numbers may not seem significant, but they reflect the frequent use of a drug that many had written off as a thing of the past. That alone concerns authorities.

PCP is called many things on the street, including "angel dust," "buck-naked," "dippers," "embalming fluid," "killer weed," "love boat," "super grass," "wack," and "rocket fuel." It is cheap and easy to find in cities, and it is spreading to suburbs and smaller communities. At its seeming best, it makes you feel like Superman. At its worst, it leads to self-harm, violence, and aggression. PCP has been linked to some horrifying acts of violence, including murder and cannibalism. What is this strange drug, and why would anyone take it?

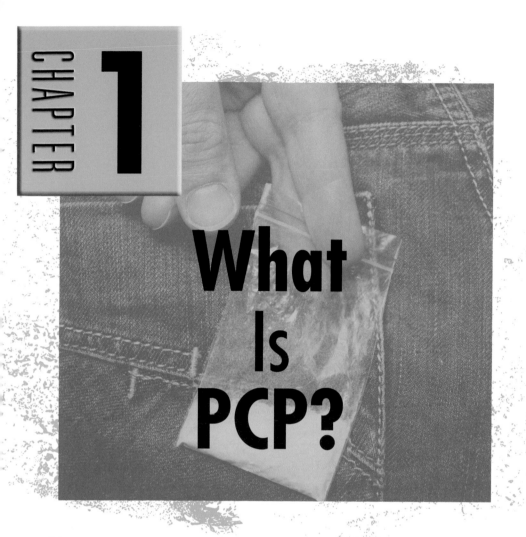

What Is PCP?

CHAPTER 1

The United States is fighting a war on drugs. According to the Drug Policy Alliance, more than $51 trillion is spent every year trying to stop this massive social problem. It seems to be a losing battle. In fact, in 2009, President Barack Obama's administration announced it would discontinue use of the phrase "war on drugs," possibly because it is a war that can't be won.

People take illegal drugs for all kinds of reasons. Some seek a form of escape from life's troubles. Others want to feel a sense of belonging, and they take drugs to be part of a crowd. And, of course, many people have become addicted to drugs, so they use because their bodies and minds crave the drugs.

Different drugs have different effects. Some are more dangerous than others. Some are easy to obtain and others aren't. Some are inexpensive, while others get people into debt. Particular drugs rise and fall in popularity. Some seem to go away forever, replaced by a newer, "better," cheaper, more accessible, or more hip and fashionable drug. PCP seemed to be one of those drugs, popular in the 1960s and 1970s, only to be replaced by something newer. Law enforcement officials

People use illegal drugs for all kinds of reasons, but by doing so, they introduce devastating problems into their lives, including addiction, illness, and even death. All of these can be avoided by simply not starting in the first place.

scratched their heads when PCP suddenly began to reemerge on the scene decades after falling out of favor.

Development of PCP

PCP is a shortened name for phencyclidine, itself a shortened version of its chemical name phenylcyclohexyl piperidine. It was originally synthesized and developed for use as a surgical anesthetic in the early-to-mid-twentieth century. When people later began to take phencyclidine recreationally, it became known as PCP.

PCP is a hallucinogen. This class of drugs includes LSD, peyote, DMT, STP, and mescaline. One reason people like to take hallucinogens is that they take you on wild, mind-altering "trips." These drugs are not commonly associated with intoxicated behavior or addiction, and there is generally not a painful period of physical withdrawal when use is discontinued. Hallucinogens have been used throughout history in religious rituals because they alter the perceptions of the users. These drugs were particularly popular during the psychedelic era of the 1960s and '70s, when people sought to "free their minds" and alter their consciousness. These people mistakenly thought there would be no permanent effects on their bodies and their brains.

PCP is illegal. It is classified as a Schedule II drug under the Controlled Substances Act. Schedule II drugs have high potential for abuse and dependence. PCP is also dangerous. Many people who take it end up severely damaged or even dead.

How Is PCP Taken?

PCP can be manufactured and produced in various forms. A bitter, white powder, it can be snorted or sprinkled on the leaves of tobacco or other herbs, rolled into a cigarette, and smoked. In tablet or capsule form, it can be swallowed. As a liquid, it can be used to coat tobacco or marijuana cigarettes and smoked.

When it was first used recreationally in the late 1960s, PCP was most often taken as a pill. In fact, the name PCP is an abbreviated form of the drug's nickname at the time, "PeaCe

PCP is a white, bitter powder. Also known as "angel dust," it can be snorted or sprinkled on tobacco or marijuana and rolled into a cigarette.

Pill." Not long after, it became popular to snort the powder form, often referred to as angel dust.

Today, one of the most popular methods of using PCP is to smoke marijuana or tobacco cigarettes dipped in liquid PCP. This is called "fry." Combined, users get the hallucinatory effects of PCP with the mellow high of marijuana or the stimulation of nicotine. Fry is cheap, easy to take, and doesn't arouse suspicion because it looks like a regular joint or cigarette. Sometimes people also dip the cigarettes in embalming fluid. Embalming fluid prolongs the burn time of the cigarette, allowing the user to experience a longer-lasting high.

Aside from being addictive, fry has many physical and psychiatric hazards. Because of the PCP contained within, it can produce cravings and dependence, stunt growth in adolescents, produce the symptoms of schizophrenia, lead to long-term memory loss, and cause depression, among other things. Users can become violent or suicidal. Potential physical effects from embalming fluid are bronchitis, brain damage, lung damage, and loss of coordination. The marijuana in fry affects coordination, promotes hallucinations, impairs respiratory function, elevates heart rate, and increases the occurrence of certain cancers. Fry is extremely dangerous.

Manufacture and Trafficking

Most of the world's supply of PCP is produced in the United States. Nearly all of this is manufactured illegally in underground laboratories. PCP is easy to manufacture; almost anyone can learn to put it together without needing chemi-cal expertise. Its ingredients are fairly easy to obtain and don't raise a red flag when purchased. No special equipment is involved. It's so simple to make that people mix liquid PCP using the "bucket method": they literally combine the ingre-dients in large buckets.

The most prominent producers of PCP in the United States are urban gangs, such as the Crips and the Bloods. Most, but not all, of the production takes place in California. These gangs can easily traffic the drug to Mexico, and they also distribute it throughout the rest of the United States.

An LAPD officer arrests a member of the notorious Bloods gang. The majority of PCP in the United States is manufactured by the Bloods and their rival gang, the Crips.

The Crips, Bloods, and other gangs have vast, powerful networks in many parts of the country. They have developed very simple but effective methods of distributing the PCP that they manufacture to other urban areas, particularly Washington, D.C., Baltimore, Chicago, Houston, and New York City. They pour the liquid into inconspicuous containers, such as emptied-out sports drink and mouthwash bottles. Then they ship quantities using regular commercial carriers like buses, trains, package delivery companies, and even airlines.

Once the PCP arrives at its distribution center, it is poured into small glass vials and empty vanilla extract bottles. These are sold in targeted locations within the city, such as public housing complexes, college campuses, and parties and raves. Prices are cheap. One ounce of liquid PCP, which is quite a bit, ranges from $125 to $600. Tablets and powder cost around $20 per item or gram, respectively. PCP-laced cigarettes can be as cheap as $5 each.

TEN

1. Is PCP a "safe" drug?

2. What does taking PCP feel like?

3. What does PCP do to your body?

4. What does PCP do to your brain?

5. Can I become addicted to PCP?

6. Will my parents and teachers know I'm using PCP?

7. Can you overdose on PCP?

8. What is the treatment for PCP overdose?

9. Is PCP a natural substance?

10. Will PCP make me feel more self-confident?

2

PCP's Strange History

The drug that is manufactured in the "labs" of gangs and sold on the streets for recreational use was first manufactured for an entirely different purpose. In the early part of the twentieth century, scientists developed phencyclidine as an intravenous anesthetic to numb patients' pain during surgeries.

However, phencyclidine was far from perfect: patients experienced dramatic side effects postsurgery, including hallucinations and disorientation. The drug was marketed and used commercially as a human anesthetic in the 1950s and '60s, but similar problems forced its discontinuation. Another attempt to find a legitimate medical use for phencyclidine was its use as an anesthetic for animals during veterinary operations, but that, too, was short-lived. At the same time, chemists developed anesthetics that were free of phencyclidine's adverse side effects. It seemed that phencyclidine's days were numbered.

The Emergence of a Youth Counterculture

By the late 1960s, the United States and much of the Western world were experiencing social upheaval. In the years that followed World War II (1939–1945), America had thrived, becoming richer and more powerful than ever. At the dawn of the 1960s, President John F. Kennedy ushered in an era of hope and activism. Kennedy's youth and vitality inspired young Americans to discover their voice and take an active role in the public debates and decision making that so directly affected their lives.

When Kennedy was assassinated on November 22, 1963, America's future suddenly seemed uncertain. The next few years saw the country divided over the civil rights movement—in which many Americans fought against stiff resistance for the rights of African Americans, women, and other minorities to be treated equally—and U.S. involvement in the Vietnam War. Americans watched news stories about riots, murder, and war on their television screens. Many wondered what had happened to their country.

Hippies flocked to San Francisco in 1967 during what became known as the "Summer of Love." Free from responsibility and disillusioned by their government, they practiced free love and experimented with mind-altering drugs.

Disillusioned by the status quo and a government they believed was betraying them, many young people simply "dropped out." They dropped out of school, out of their families, and out of mainstream society. Searching for greater fulfillment, they lived together on communes and advocated peace and free love. They were called hippies and were scorned by those who adhered to tradition. In an effort to open their minds to new possibilities and paradigms, they used drugs, including marijuana and LSD.

Haight-Ashbury and the "Summer of Love"

Many of these hippies had flocked to San Francisco, specifically to an area called Haight-Ashbury. Their massive migration there in 1967 had been dubbed by journalists as the "Summer of Love." This was a massive social revolution that was fueled in part by hallucinogenic drugs and psychedelic rock music. Hallucinogens such as LSD were the drug of choice because they allowed users to go on "trips" and alter their perspectives on life, existence, and reality. They believed they were opening up new worlds of thought, feeling, experience, and spirituality.

During this time, local police, emergency professionals, and other medical personnel were wearied by the daily number of users who had overdosed or gone on "bad trips" (bad drug experiences) and required treatment. It was at the Haight-Ashbury Free Medical Clinic that doctors first saw the very serious side effects of phencyclidine taken recreationally.

What at first seemed like the influence of a bad batch of LSD turned out to be the typical

The Haight Ashbury Free Medical Clinic treated the first cases of recreational phencyclidine abuse. The clinic had been established to treat the swelling population of hippies in San Francisco during the Summer of Love.

effects of phencyclidine. The drug had been manufactured into a convenient tablet form and was known as the PeaCe Pill (PCP for short) on the street. Those people who had taken the drug exhibited strange, often violent, behavior.

The Summer of Love ended, and many of its participants abandoned Haight-Ashbury due to the crime and widespread drug use that had overtaken the neighborhood. Others left to lead more "normal" lives. The doctors at the free clinic assumed that the hippies who remained would stick with marijuana and LSD, the two drugs that really defined the hippie experience. They thought PCP would fall by the wayside, especially given its harsh side effects.

Angel Dust

You can't blame doctors for incorrectly predicting that they would not see cases of PCP overdose for much longer. Unlike the romanticized stereotype of the "mellow" feeling some users experience when smoking marijuana or the vivid, colorful, mind-altering effects of LSD, the bad trip of PCP was harsh, violent, and often terrifying. Nevertheless, by the 1970s, PCP use was fairly widespread. Its use might not have been as common as some other drugs, but it was still popular enough to be a problem—a big problem, according to many law enforcement and public health officials. A 1978 interview in *People* magazine conducted with a San Francisco drug expert referred to PCP as the "most dangerous drug to hit the streets since LSD." The method of taking PCP shifted; rather than taking

This is a colorized microscopic slide of crystallized angel dust.

PeaCe Pills, users now smoked or snorted it. The most common street name for PCP at this time was "angel dust." This was because the drug appeared most commonly in powder form. It was said that when the liquid dried, it looked like angel dust.

No one could quite understand PCP's popularity. It made users violent and aggressive, and they couldn't even remember having used the drug. One reason it was still in existence was the fact that it was easy to get. PCP is simple and inexpensive to manufacture. That meant it was readily available and affordable. It didn't seem to be addictive or do much harm. But on the other hand, the high it gave wasn't superior to other drugs, such as marijuana or heroin. In fact, it could be quite harsh, not a "high" at all.

PCP use peaked in the late 1970s and dropped dramatically after that. Legal manufacturing of phencyclidine was stopped in 1978 because of its abuse as a street drug, so it became difficult to obtain. In addition, PCP's popularity was eclipsed by drugs with less bizarre side effects, like cocaine. Finally, a cheaper and more effective drug took its place: crack, the freebase form of cocaine, which can be smoked. Crack is easy to score on the street and gives users a short but intense high. The crack epidemic devastated U.S. urban areas beginning in the mid-1980s and showed no signs of stopping.

A Comeback of Sorts

Almost fifty years after the first reported recreational use of PCP, the drug suddenly reappeared once more. It seemed that just when authorities began to gain traction in the war on crack, PCP again poked its head up into the open drug market. The number of PCP users was not especially significant when compared to other, more prevalent drugs. Nevertheless, authorities were concerned about the increase in use of an illegal substance they thought they'd vanquished once and for all. In many U.S. cities, the number

DRUG SEIZURE!

On February 15, 2012, authorities in Los Angeles seized more than 130 gallons (492 liters) of PCP. They also uncovered ingredients and cash that would have produced a whopping 500 additional gallons (1,893 l). The trail led authorities to a local gang member who was making and trafficking the drug across the country. One hundred thirty gallons (492 l) of PCP yields about ten million doses. At an average of $10 a pop, the street value of the manufactured PCP was almost $100 million!

of criminal defendants who tested positive for PCP has increased steadily over the past decade.

Why has PCP gained popularity after seemingly dying a quick death so many years ago? Authorities say the chief reasons are the availability and the price. PCP is now made on the street. The ingredients used to manufacture PCP are fairly common and the drug is not difficult to manufacture. Many illegal drugs require a vast knowledge of chemistry to manufacture, and users pay the price for ingredients and the expertise that went into making the drug. PCP can be man-ufactured with very little expertise. This is reflected in the street price, which is very low. PCP is an affordable high even for adolescents, although manufacturers still manage to make considerable profits on the production and trade of the drug.

PCP Today

Now that PCP has made a comeback, its prevalence is expected to increase, albeit slowly. Its emergence began in urban areas of the United States, namely Los Angeles, Washington, D.C., Houston, and Baltimore, but has spread to even more cities. Chiefly manufactured by urban gangs, it can be delivered or shipped anywhere in the country. It has already made appearances in suburbs and is beginning to encroach upon small towns. PCP is sold and used on the streets, but there is evidence that it is also invading rave culture.

New York City's police commissioner speaks at a press conference announcing the NYPD's indictment of a large-scale drug ring responsible for the production and sale of PCP. After many years of dormancy, PCP sales and use have risen, particular in major U.S. cities.

Is PCP destined to fade away again in a few years, the eventual victim of a newer, better, cheaper drug? Will today's adolescents turn away from it once they see that its dangers far outweigh its pleasures? Only time will tell, but one thing is for sure: If people knew the adverse effects—some of them long-term—of taking PCP even once, they would never experiment with it in the first place.

3

The Social Dangers of PCP

W hen you abuse a drug—any drug—there are potentially grave consequences. Whether it's a one-time experiment or something that turns into a habit, all illegal drugs have the potential for life-changing danger and destruction. Serious drug abuse doesn't just harm the user, however. It can also damage the user's support circle, including friends and family.

Ruining the lives of yourself, your friends, and your family members might seem like nobody's business but your own, but

24

there is someone else who is affected by your drug habits: the rest of us. According to DrugAbuse.gov, the abuse of illegal drugs—and even alcohol and tobacco—costs Americans more than $600 billion per year. How can this be? Why doesn't this kind of abuse cost the user only? The answer is that when people abuse drugs and alcohol, they get arrested, hurt, and unmotivated. The tab Americans are picking up is for costs relating to crime, health care, and lost work productivity.

A Drain on Law Enforcement Resources

Statistics show that the influence of drugs and alcohol can directly result in criminal and violent behavior. According to Bureau of Justice statistics calculated from a recent survey of prisoners in state and federal correctional facilities, 32 percent of state and 26 percent of federal inmates had committed their crimes while using illegal drugs. As far as the prisoners held in jail, 29 percent of convicted prisoners reported committing their offense while under the influence of illegal drugs. Sometimes these prisoners committed a crime to get money to pay for their drug habit. Other times the influence of illegal substances caused them to engage in criminal behavior that they wouldn't normally undertake.

Statistically, the link between criminal activity and PCP use specifically is difficult to discern. First, PCP is often lumped in with other hallucinogens, such as LSD, in research. Also, because PCP had a low profile for so long and made its comeback only fairly recently, there have been few

There is a strong connection between criminal behavior and illegal drugs, such as PCP. Many crimes are committed under the influence of drugs, and many offenders commit crimes in order to pay for drugs.

current studies exploring how PCP use does or doesn't result in criminal activity. Nevertheless, there are enough anecdotal police reports and stories in the media for us to reach the conclusion that there is indeed a strong connection.

As with most illegal drugs, PCP use is a burden on our criminal justice system. The so-called war on drugs costs the U.S. economy more than $193 billion per year, according to a recent U.S. Department of Justice study. The most significant costs are associated with spending on police resources, court personnel, prison guards, and officials who track, arrest, try, and imprison drug users, sellers, and traffickers.

When people take PCP, it may well be that they can do so quietly in their home without attracting the attention of police. Chronic use, however, may lead to criminal behavior. When the police are called, they must spend time apprehending the PCP user, calming or subduing and handcuffing him or her, and taking the user to the station or hospital. Not only does that cost taxpayers, but it also diverts police resources that could be better spent on other public safety and law enforcement measures.

Medical Resources

Many PCP users who draw the attention of law enforcement require medical assistance. Sometimes they injure themselves in the course of their PCP trip. They do not feel pain from the injury because PCP causes users to feel no pain, but they must be admitted to the emergency room for treatment. Other times there is simply the potential to harm themselves or others.

Regardless, it is a group effort among emergency room personnel and law enforcement to keep PCP users as calm as possible and subdue and confine them so that they will not harm themselves or others. This involves restraining the user, usually with handcuffs or restraints connected to a gurney.

Since PCP's high lasts six to eight hours, and because the drug can can stay in the body's system for up to forty-eight hours, users must be restrained for several hours until any imminent danger of violence or self-harm appears to have passed. During this time, hospital personnel must keep a close eye on the patient and

A police detective watches over a PCP abuser he has arrested. PCP can cause users to feel superhuman and extremely strong. This challenges police and hospital personnel, who often must restrain users until the chemicals have exited their systems.

endure yelling, threats, and insults hurled at them by the disorderly user.

According to the Drug Abuse Action Network's (DAWN) recent national estimates of drug-related emergency room visits, 2.1 million hospital visits were medical emergencies involving drug abuse. Forty-seven percent of those visits were related to an illicit drug. The most common drug involved in these visits was cocaine, at 43.4 percent. By contrast, PCP is lumped in as an "other" drug, along with other hallucinogens, at less than 4 percent. There are no available statistics representing the victims of PCP users who required medical attention.

PCP AND THE ENVIRONMENT

Phencyclidine is made from toxic ingredients, including ether. The manufacture of PCP results in waste that must be disposed of. When legitimate operations need to dispose of hazardous substances, they contract qualified toxic waste management companies. These licensed companies follow guidelines established by the Environmental Protection Agency (EPA) to safely dispose of such substances without harming the environment. Street gangs involved in illegal activity, however, are unlikely to follow the same precautions.

The result is the careless and illegal disposal of hazardous materials into our environment. According to the Drug Enforcement Administration (DEA), ether is highly flammable and explosive. Another PCP ingredient, phenyl magnesium bromide, reacts explosively if it comes into contact with water. Sodium cyanide is a deadly poison.

Illegal PCP labs often dump their waste in populated areas, unbeknownst to those around them. Under the wrong conditions, unsuspecting individuals and nearby residents could be exposed to dangerous and even deadly fumes or a tainted water supply.

Reinforcing the Power of Gangs

When PCP reemerged as a recreational drug, it was no longer regulated and government-approved, but instead was produced on the streets by amateurs. Specifically, the manufacture of this "new" PCP was overseen by urban gangs, such as the Crips and the Bloods (who are bitter and violent rivals). Because PCP is relatively easy to produce and doesn't require serious chemical expertise, and because its ingredients are fairly accessible, street gangs can manufacture it quickly and cheaply. Once the drug is

A police officer handcuffs a gang member during a drug sweep. Nationally networked gangs have taken over the production and sale of PCP. Police departments have begun to target such gangs to eliminate the street drug.

manufactured, members of these well-established gangs are in a uniquely convenient position to traffic PCP on their own streets and throughout nationwide networks.

Drugs are predominantly trafficked by urban gangs in larger metropolitan areas of the United States. However, drug activity controlled by gangs in suburbs and small towns has increased. The purchase of PCP and other drugs helps support these gangs. According to the Department of Justice, the selling of illegal drugs and weapons, along with illegal activities such as prostitution, can bring in millions of dollars every month to these gangs.

The money that users spend on drugs only makes gangs more powerful, better armed, and more violent and lethal. It means they can fund a stronger and more widespread network of drug trafficking and other illegal activities. It also enables them to launch new illegal ventures that are corrosive to neighborhoods, towns, cities, and all of society. Many gangs buy up real estate and legitimate local businesses like barber shops, tattoo parlors, and restaurants. These places are convenient locations from which they can sell their drug supplies. Consequently, many urban neighborhoods are essentially owned and controlled by gangs. Meanwhile, these gangs profit from legal and illegal ventures as they continue their reigns of violence, terror, and indoctrination.

When gangs have more power, they threaten society. Not only do they engage in violence, robbery, prostitution, and drug trafficking, but they also destroy the potential of young minds. First, they introduce PCP and other drugs to young kids and encourage them to become dependent on them. They make gang life look appealing in order to get these kids to join their criminal operations, or they use the threat of physical violence to coerce them. Before long, these kids must sell drugs themselves to stay in the gang. Once they are in the gang, it is very difficult to get out—both because it can seem financially lucrative to stay in and because it can be physically dangerous, even fatal, to try to leave.

A Threat to Citizens

One of the potentially ruinous effects of increased PCP abuse on our society is less dramatic but just as grave. Compared with adolescents who do not use drugs, teen PCP users are more likely to drop out of school and remain unemployed or have difficulty staying employed. PCP users have difficulty focusing on learning and working, and, as a result, it becomes nearly impossible to be a productive member of society.

For a society to be successful, all citizens must contribute as much as they can, providing whatever it is they have to offer. When young people drop out of school and cannot hold down a job because of their drug habit, they are no longer productive members of society. Because their contributions are minimal to nonexistent—in fact, they may be costing their community— they are a drain on public resources. They are also directly undermining and devaluing the potential of our society.

When people become consumed with taking PCP or any drug to the point that they can't stay in school; hold a job; be a good neighbor, friend, or family member; or take proper care of their children, they are not contributing to society. Indeed, they are contributing to its breakdown.

MYTHS & FACTS

MYTH PCP is not addictive.

FACT You may have been told that one of the reasons you should take PCP is that you won't become addicted to it. But PCP is addictive. Taking it can create psychological dependence. Especially after repeated use, you may crave the drug and exhibit compulsive behavior with the goal of getting more of it. In addition, users need to increase their dosages over time because they develop a tolerance for the drug.

MYTH Milk can counteract the effects of PCP.

FACT There are rumors circulating that claim milk is an antidote for PCP symptoms. If only it were that easy! There is no truth to this claim. In fact, there is no known antidote to counter the toxicity of PCP. Often the most successful treatment is to calm the user and let the drug pass through his or her system. Emergency room doctors often help calm extremely violent patients admitted with symptoms of PCP use by administering Valium or Haldol.

MYTH PCP turns you into a violent, murderous monster.

FACT PCP gains a lot of media attention because many of the most bizarre crimes seem to have been committed by people high on PCP. It is true that the drug can cause you to behave in ways you never would normally, and it can lead to psychotic behavior. There are many news stories that describe grisly acts of violence and murder. However, these incidences are by no means the majority of PCP users' experiences. It may be that the violent individuals already have exhibited behavioral problems and that the drug is not the primary cause of it.

4

PCP's Effects on the Brain and Body

P CP use takes a toll on its users, physically, mentally, and behaviorally. Effects can vary depending on the person, dose, and term of use. In general, people who take PCP experience perceptual distortions and hallucinatory effects. They also feel as if they are disassociated from their surrounding environment. Long-term abuse can result in brain damage or impairment, especially if it is taken with other drugs. PCP also affects users' behavior. It impairs their judgment, causing them to take unnecessary risks. Their actions can be unpredictable, and they may also become violent.

Variations in Dosage

The effects of PCP on a person differ dramatically depending on the dose. Users generally aim for low to moderate doses (1 mg to 5 mg), which result in a carefree state and a feeling of dreamy floating. These doses cause fairly harmless physical symptoms that users barely notice. They may exhibit slurred speech and move their eyes rapidly. Their coordination suffers, and they may walk oddly or bump into things. Users do begin to feel slightly detached from their surroundings.

As people increase their dosage, they experience more severe dissociation, disorientation, and confusion. They also have mood swings and partial amnesia. Increasingly, they are unable to feel pain.

The effects of higher doses of PCP—10 mg or more—are more dramatic. Users experience visual and auditory

The effects of PCP vary depending on the dose. Moderate doses can have catatonic effects, but just a slightly higher dose can bring on aggressive behavior.

hallucinations and appear catatonic (staring blankly). But it is the feelings obtained from these levels of PCP that can get users into trouble. Users believe they have superhuman strength and have unlimited abilities. Combine that with the anxiety, aggression, hostility, and paranoia they may also feel, and mix in the poor judgment and inability to feel pain that comes at this dose, and the potential for danger increases dramatically. Users who hop in the car while high on PCP may speed and drive erratically. Others may jump out a window, believing they can fly. Others pick fights or punch walls. People who take high doses of PCP do things they would never ordinarily do. And sometimes it leads to their death.

Regular users of PCP need to increase their dosage levels and frequency to experience the high they felt when they first began taking the drug. Generally, new users feel the effects of PCP in the first five minutes. The high stays with them from four to six hours. PCP may stay in the system for up to forty-eight hours. Once a person becomes a chronic user, say a few days a week for two or three months with higher doses, it might take several years for the PCP to leave their system. It may take even longer for their body and brain to return to normal functioning.

Physical Effects of PCP Use

As with abuse of alcohol and other drugs, taking PCP results in a type of intoxication. The entire cycle can last from twenty-four to forty-eight hours and can be roughly divided into three phases. While the last phase is the gravest and can lead to death through organ failure, for example, it is actually the first two phases that are more dangerous. This is because accidents and suicide are more likely in these first two phases.

In the first phase, known as behavioral toxicity, users experience elevated body temperature, heart rate, and respiration (breathing). They may drool or even vomit. Their eyes dart back and forth, but they seem to stare blankly. They cannot control their muscles.

The next phase, the stuporous phase, is so named because the user is in a stupor. Body temperature, heart rate, and respiration increase even more. Muscles become stiff, and the user may begin twitching or have a seizure if he or she is stimulated.

In the comatose stage, or final phase, the user is actually in a deep coma. This period can last from one to four days. Instead of darting, the eyes drift and the pupils are dilated. Body temperature rises so much that the person sweats profusely. Heart rate is elevated to even higher levels—dangerously high levels. Respiration may stop. The user does not feel pain.

The general list of physical symptoms associated with PCP use are as follows:

- involuntary rapid movements of the eyes
- high blood pressure
- racing heartbeat
- dizziness and shakiness
- drooling

- increased body temperature
- reduced response to pain
- slurred speech
- exaggerated gait
- excessive sensitivity to sound
- dilated pupils
- skin dryness and redness
- muscle rigidity or frozen posture
- seizures
- breakdown of muscle and excretion of muscle proteins in urine
- coma
- loss of coordination despite the illusion of strength and invulnerability

Psychological and Neurological Effects

PCP affects your brain and your nervous system. Because there are many other factors involved in PCP use, however, it is difficult to isolate the neurological effects of the drug. This is because people who take PCP often abuse alcohol and other drugs as well, and are involved in accidents as a result of their PCP use. Also, it can be difficult to determine cause and effect: people who take PCP are more inclined to abuse other drugs and to behave irresponsibly.

There have not been studies isolating the effects of PCP use in humans. Still, research has shown damage to the cortex

ROBO-TRIPPING

Even though PCP is inexpensive and fairly easily available, many teens have turned to an even more accessible and legal drug that has similar effects. For the last decade, adolescent recreational use of over-the-counter (OTC) cough and cold pills has reached epidemic proportions.

Users call these pills "skittles" or "triple Cs," and they call the action of taking them "robo-tripping." Robo-tripping is appealing to teen drug users because it is legal, affordably priced, and easily accessible.

Most of these medications contain the active ingredient dextromethorphan (DXM), a cough suppressant. DXM is safe in regular doses, but if taken in large quantities, it can produce many of the effects of PCP. At low doses, DMX produces a pleasant "buzz." But most teens graduate to larger doses—generally an entire box of pills—for a more intense experience. These large quantities cause hallucinations, tremors, and slurred speech. Extremely large doses can result in seizures and even death.

There are psychological dangers as well. Heavy users become dependent on DXM, often doing whatever is necessary to obtain more of the substance for a fix. Many teens report stealing the pills or the money to buy the pills. They also admit that they began to lose control of their lives, including failing grades and losing interest in other activities, once they began robo-tripping.

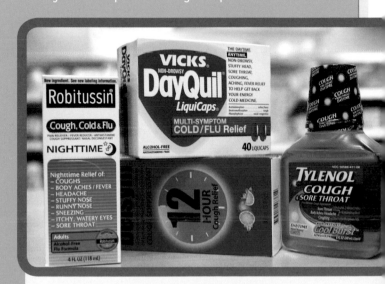

These over-the-counter cold and cough remedies are often abused by teens and other users looking for a legally obtainable and inexpensive high that mimics the effects of PCP.

(an area of the brain) in rats that were given PCP, and the same might hold true for humans. Animals exposed to PCP also had difficulty learning and remembering.

Psychiatric and social symptoms exhibited by even casual PCP users include hallucinations of a sensory (touch), visual (seeing), and auditory (hearing) nature; confusion; disorientation; dissociation from their environment; and paranoia. Users also experience dramatic mood swings. They start out feeling pleasant, then become agitated, anxious, aggressive, and enraged.

PCP users are impulsive and unpredictable. They have bad judgment. Their memories become impaired. They begin to display symptoms akin to schizophrenia. If they stop using the drug abruptly, they can become severely depressed.

Effects on Long-Term PCP Users

Although even first-timers court danger when they use PCP, chronic (long-term) users face severe physical and psychiatric side effects that can take months, years, or even a lifetime to heal. As mentioned, serious PCP users exhibit symptoms of schizophrenia, a serious brain disorder in which patients cannot interpret reality normally. While chronic PCP users do not "get" schizophrenia, they do experience hallucinations, delusions, and paranoid behavior, all of which are symptoms of schizophrenia.

Some of the physical and psychiatric symptoms of PCP use that occur in casual users persist for some time in long-term users. After several months of use, and even after they stop taking PCP altogether, people suffer from memory loss, confused thoughts, and impaired speech for a prolonged period of time. Teens who take the drug chronically have a special set of challenges. Excessive PCP use may stunt growth hormones, preventing teen users from reaching their full height. Also, PCP use may impair their learning processes.

Long-term users of all ages face social problems that result from becoming addicted to PCP. Most have difficulty maintaining relationships. In their quest to obtain more PCP, they may cut ties with or steal from parents, friends, and other family members who do not share their drug habit. They also lose control of their lives, making poor decisions, falling into criminal activity, and exposing themselves to disease and high-risk lifestyles. This chaos makes it difficult to function at school or hold down a job. Many chronic users drop out of school and have a hard time staying employed. This creates a host of financial problems that add to their already desperate circumstances.

Behavioral Effects

One of the most dangerous effects of PCP use is the way it makes users behave. PCP causes users to feel invincible, as if there is nothing they can't do. It also makes them extremely agitated. Finally, it blocks their ability to feel pain. Together, these factors create an environment for potentially extreme harm.

When people take PCP, they often think they can fly like a bird or operate a car like a NASCAR driver or throw a punch like a prizefighter. They engage in risky behavior because it doesn't seem risky to them. And if they happen to get hurt, they don't feel it. Therefore, under the influence of PCP, simple activities like driving and swimming can become dangerous to the user and others.

There is no shortage of videos on YouTube that show the frightening behavior of people who have taken PCP. Some can be seen wandering down a freeway naked (PCP makes the body temperature rise so much that users often feel the need to remove their clothes) as cars slam on their brakes to avoid an accident. Others can be seen howling like animals and destroying fences and shrubbery. These people almost always wind up in the emergency room and come to the next day

PCP users often howl like animals, become aggressive, and, in some cases, demonstrate violent and psychotic behavior.

with no memory of their behavior or why they are in such severe pain and under arrest.

Some experts argue that PCP use is directly linked to social violence. The media has reported several dramatic stories of people who took PCP and committed horrible acts of violence. For example, in 2002, rapper Big Lurch was convicted of murdering his roommate and eating part of her lung while high on PCP. A thirty-three-year old New Jersey woman decapitated her own son while under the influence of PCP. There are many more similarly grisly stories, causing people to believe that PCP drives its users to murder and cannibalism.

Whether PCP alone is to blame in these atrocious acts, as opposed to being one among several contributing factors, such as preexisting mental illness, is unknown. It's impossible to determine if these people would have committed these or similar acts of violence if they were not taking PCP at the time. Regardless, there are enough terrible and true stories surrounding PCP use that no one should ever feel safe trying it, not even once.

5

Abuse
and
Recovery

C hronic use of PCP can result in addiction. Symptoms of dependency may be less physical in nature than psychological and social. There are no controlled studies on PCP addiction in humans, so it is uncertain whether or not chronic users experience physical along with psychological addiction and withdrawal. Studies show, however, that monkeys introduced to PCP repeatedly give themselves doses of the drug to maintain a continuous state of intoxication. If the drug is taken away, they exhibit physical as well as psychological withdrawal symptoms. The good news is that if properly diagnosed and confronted, PCP addiction is treatable.

PCP Addiction

PCP use imposes a viselike grip on its users. What begins as harmless recreational use can quickly develop into an addicted lifestyle over which the user loses all control. As with all illegal drug use, there is an element of dependence, whether physical, emotional, or psychological. The user begins to need the drug—or the lifestyle that accompanies it—on a regular basis. Some substances, like cocaine, heroin, and nicotine, create cravings in the system so that the user cannot get through his or her day without another dose. He or she feels physically ill without a fix. The only way to feel better is to get more of the substance. This results in regular, habitual use.

Other drugs do not generate such strong cravings, but they can be addictive nonetheless. Regardless of the degree to which PCP use results in physical addiction, users do become dependent on it. Experts warn that it is dangerous to write off PCP as a substance that is not addictive. Why else, they argue, would people continue to use it?

As with most illegal substances, trying PCP even once can change your life for the worse. Some people turn to PCP as a form of escape. They want to feel invincible even for a short time, so they take PCP. A few hours of forgetting their troubles can create new ones, however. Instead of escaping from life's problems,

As euphoric as a PCP high may feel, coming down is not as pleasant. PCP users may continue taking the drug in a futile attempt to recapure the first experience of the high, resulting in addiction.

they end up digging themselves into an even deeper hole.

It is a slippery slope for the recreational user who wants to experiment with PCP. One or two evenings of fun can rapidly spiral downward into a lifetime of trouble. The person who thinks PCP is safe to try because it's not as addictive as heroin or methamphetamines is dead wrong. PCP may not be as addictive as those substances and it might show up in news reports less frequently, but it can certainly take you down the same treacherous and deadly road.

Let's say you take PCP one Saturday night with your friends. Maybe nothing bad happens; you just have a good time. Everyone forgets about the upcoming test at school and about the fight that they had with their parents or boyfriend or girlfriend. Instead, you all feel strong, like nothing can stop you. That feeling of power and invincibility was the highlight of your week. So why not try it again next Saturday? And then the next Saturday, and after school on Tuesday. Soon you begin to increase the dosage. The next thing you know, you have a dependency problem.

PCP causes you to do things you normally would never even dream of doing. Perhaps one night you and your friends take PCP and decide it would be a good idea to break into the neighbors' house. It will be totally harmless because you know they're not home. You just want to take a look around. While you're there, you see some jewelry and some cash and steal it. Suddenly, you're guilty of breaking and entering, as well as theft.

Or maybe you decide to take a ride around town after you've taken PCP. You think you're fine to drive, but PCP impairs your judgment and makes you very reckless. Before you know it, you've totaled your parents' car and caused injury to yourself, your passengers, someone in another car, or pedestrians. Hopefully no one died. You could end up at the hospital or in jail.

And here is where the slippery slope can start. Without professional help and a strong conviction to stop using PCP, you might keep on doing it. This will lead to trouble at school. With your grades tanking, you might drop out. Even if you get a dead-end job, your erratic behavior and undependability could make you lose it. After daily fights with your parents, you move out of the house. Your friends start to become annoyed by you and no longer trust you to tell the truth and not hit them up for money or steal from them.

PCP addiction can lead to irresponsible, erratic behavior, including criminal acts. To obtain the money to pay for more drugs, addicts often rob and steal.

Suddenly you have no one to help you, nowhere to live. In order to pay for your PCP, you are forced to steal. If you hurt yourself, you can't afford the hospital bill. The PCP itself isn't your only problem, but it is a problem that creates many others. It's affecting your health, your relationships and friendships, your mental stability, your safety, and your future.

This scenario sounds extreme. However, the reality is, that no one knows where that first use of PCP will take him or her.

HOW TO FIND HELP

If you or someone you know is addicted to PCP or another substance, it is important to understand that help is available. Talk to someone you know or trust and ask for help. Sometimes that is the hardest part. Admitting the problem to a parent, teacher, doctor, or minister is a good start. They can direct you to resources in your area. To have the best chance of quitting, find a good program administered by caring and experienced addiction counselors and mental health professionals.

You could be the person who tries it once or twice and has no adverse effects, or you could be the one whose life gets ruined in short order.

Not only can escalated PCP use lead to erratic behavior that results in dangerous or criminal acts, it can also harm you in other ways. Unless you manufacture it yourself, you don't know exactly what is in the PCP you ingest, snort, or smoke. If you can't be sure that taking PCP won't affect you adversely, perhaps fatally, why would you willingly try it? It's like playing Russian roulette. The risk is just too great.

Diagnosing PCP Dependency

The American Psychiatric Association divides PCP disorders into two classes: dependence and abuse. Both can be difficult to diagnose because it is nearly impossible to isolate PCP symptoms from other factors. Very few PCP users are taking that drug only; most abuse other drugs as well. The symptoms also can vary in kind and intensity from one user to another. Some exhibit no symptoms whatsoever, while others show definite signs of PCP dependence and withdrawal. Prior psychological problems also play a role. People who have preexisting mental health or psychiatric issues are more likely to experience extreme or alarming side effects from taking PCP.

Treatment

Immediate treatment for people who have recently taken PCP consists of calming them down and possibly restraining them to ensure the safety of themselves and others. Often emergency

Treatment for PCP addiction has proven to be very successful. Therapists and counselors can help addicts understand why they crave PCP and how to break the craving-and-using cycle of addiction. They can also help addicts get their lives back on track.

room doctors administer Valium in an effort to relax the patient. However, no medication has yet been found that halts the effects of PCP. Time is the only antidote to PCP, and the user should be kept calm and confined until the drug has run its course and is out of his or her system.

Chronic, long-term PCP users often need antipsychotic medication because extended abuse can result in symptoms that resemble or mimic schizophrenia. If the patient seems to be depressed, antidepressants may be administered and outpatient therapy sessions are prescribed.

If someone really wants to break the chains of psychological dependence upon PCP, he or she must have a strong support network. Often the family and friends who make up that network must convince the PCP abuser that he or she has a problem and should get help for it. Once the user admits the problem, the hard work begins. Private sessions with therapists and self-help programs such as Narcotics Anonymous can be helpful, as can admission into rehabilitation facilities. Many users relapse but eventually have success once they realize that they need to change their lifestyle.

The easiest way to treat an addiction is to avoid developing it in the first place. PCP use is in no way worth the trouble it can cause.

GLOSSARY

addiction The continued use of a substance to the point of dependence.

antidote Medicine taken to counteract the effects of another drug.

behavioral toxicity Abnormalities in behavior caused by drugs.

catatonic A state marked by rigidity and lack of movement.

chronic Long-term or recurring.

comatose stage The final phase of PCP intoxication, during which the user is actually in a coma.

dissociation The state of being separated or disconnected.

DXM An ingredient in many cough suppressants that mimics the effects of PCP.

fry The street term for marijuana or tobacco cigarettes that are dipped in PCP and sometimes embalming fluid and then dried and smoked.

hallucinogen A type of drug that causes hallucinations (altered perception or sensory input that doesn't correspond to reality).

illicit Illegal.

intoxication A state induced by alcohol, drugs, and poisons characterized by physical and cognitive impairment.

invincible Unable to be conquered.

neurological Related to the body's nerves and nervous system.

perception distortions Seeing something in a way that doesn't strictly correspond to reality.

propagate To reproduce.

relapse To backtrack or use drugs again after a period of abstinence and sobriety.

respiration The act of breathing.

satiate To make full or satisfied.

seizure A sudden attack (as of disease); the physical manifestations (such as convulsions, sensory disturbances, or loss of consciousness) resulting from abnormal electrical discharges in the brain.

stuporous phase The second phase of PCP intoxication, marked by dazed appearance, rigidity, and elevated temperature, heart rate, and respiration.

withdrawal The physical and psychological symptoms that occur after the abrupt discontinuation of a drug or other addictive substance.

FOR MORE INFORMATION

American Addiction Centers
115 East Park Drive, 2nd Floor
Brentwood, TN 37207
(877) 586-7128
Web site: http://www.americanaddictioncenters
.com
American Addiction Centers offer help, support, and guidance to addicts of all kinds.
The Web site offers a live chat with a rep-
resentative, as well as resource material for
the addict, loved ones, and coworkers. A
toll-free number is available for asking questions, and the organization promises that
those who complete the ninety-day program will remain clean. If they don't, they
are given a complimentary additional thirty
days of services.

Canadian Centre on Drug Abuse
75 Albert Street, Suite 500
Ottawa, ON KIP 5E7
Canada
(613) 235-4048
Web site: http://www.ccsa.ca
The Centre on Drug Abuse works to reduce
alcohol- and drug-related harm.

Drug Enforcement Administration (DEA)
800 K Street NW, Suite 500
Washington, DC 20001
(202) 305-8500
Web site: http://www.justice.gov/dea
The mission of the DEA is to enforce the controlled sub-
    stances laws and regulations of the United States and bring
    to the criminal and civil justice system of the United States
    those gangs and organizations involved in the growth, man-
    ufacture, or distribution of controlled substances appearing
    in or destined for illicit traffic in the United States; and to
    recommend and support nonenforcement programs aimed
    at reducing the availability of illicit controlled substances on
    the domestic and international markets.

Drug Policy Alliance
131 West 33rd Street, 15th Floor
New York, NY 10001
(212) 613-8020
Web site: http://www.drugpolicy.org
The Drug Policy Alliance aims to advance policies and atti-
    tudes that best reduce the harm of both drug use and
    drug prohibition.

Narcotics Anonymous (NA)
P.O. Box 9999
Van Nuys, CA 91409

(818) 773-9999

Web site: http://www.na.org

Narcotics Anonymous is the largest international twelve-step
    program serving as a supportive community for those
    recovering from drug addiction.

National Institute on Drug Abuse (NIDA)

Office of Science Policy and Communications, Public
    Information and Liaison Branch

6001 Executive Boulevard

Room 5213, MSC 9561

Bethesda, MD 20892-9561

(301) 443-1124

Web site: http://www.drugabuse.gov

The NIDA supports research to prevent and treat drug
    abuse and addiction and mitigate the impact of their
    consequences, which include the spread of HIV/AIDS
    and other infectious diseases.

Royal Canadian Mounted Police (RCMP) Drug Enforcement
    Branch

RCMP National Headquarters

Headquarters Building

73 Leikin Drive

Ottawa, ON K1A 0R2

Canada

(613) 825-1391

Web site: http://www.rcmp-grc.gc.ca/de-pd
The RCMP's drug program aims to prevent drug-related social
and economic harm by reducing the supply of and demand
for illicit drugs in Canada.

Substance Abuse and Mental Health Services Administration
(SAMSA)
1 Choke Cherry Road
Rockville, MD 20857
(877) SAMHSA-7 [72672-7]
Web site: http://www.samhsa.gov
SAMHSA's mission is to reduce the impact of substance abuse
and mental illness on America's communities.

Web Sites

Due to the changing nature of Internet links, Rosen Publishing
has developed an online list of Web sites related to the subject
of this book. This site is updated regularly. Please use this link to
access the list:

http://www.rosenlinks.com/DAC/PCPs

FOR FURTHER READING

Edelfield, Bruce, and Tracey J. Moosa. *Drug Abuse.*
New York, NY: Rosen Classroom, 2011.

Gillard, Arthur, ed. *Drug Abuse.* Detroit, MI:
Greenhaven Press, 2013.

Harmon, Daniel E. *Hallucinogens: The Dangers
of Distorted Reality.* New York, NY: Rosen
Publishing Group, 2009.

Hiber, Amanda. *Gangs.* Detroit, MI: Greenhaven
Press, 2013.

Marcovitz, Hal. *Gangs.* Edina, MN: ABDO
Publishing Company, 2010.

Marcovitz, Hal. *PCP.* Detroit, MI: Lucent Books, 2006.

McCage, Crystal. *Hallucinogens: Drugs.* San Diego,
CA: ReferencePoint Press, 2007.

Nelson, Sheila. *Hallucinogens: Unreal Visions.*
Broomall, PA: Mason Crest Publishers, 2012.

Newton, Michael. *Drug Enforcement Administration.*
New York, NY: Chelsea House Publishers, 2012.

Reagan, J. P. *PCP Dependence: Facts and Treatment
Options.* Seattle, WA: CreateSpace, 2011.

Santella, Thomas. *Hallucinogens.* New York, NY:
Chelsea House Publishers, 2012.

U.S. Department of Justice. *Drugs of Abuse.* Seattle,
WA: CreateSpace, 2012.

Willis, Laurie. *Gangs.* Detroit, MI: Greenhaven
Press, 2009.

BIBLIOGRAPHY

Associated Press. "Aspiring Rapper Who Killed
   Roommate and Ate Her Lung Sentenced to
   Life." InvisionFree.com, November 8, 2003.
   Retrieved May 2013 (http://invisionfree.com/
   forums/Forum_Talk/ar/t1647.htm).

Becker, Gary S., and Kevin M. Murphy. "Have We
   Lost the War on Drugs?" *Wall Street Journal*,
   January 4, 2013. Retrieved May 2013 (http://
   online.wsj.com/article/SB1000142412788732
   4374004578217682305605070.html).

Brenner, Lisa. "This Is What $100 Million Worth of
   PCP Looks Like." Southern California Public
   Radio, February 17, 2012. Retrieved May 2013
   (http://www.scpr.org/blogs/news/2012/02/17/
   4739/what-100000-million-pcp-looks).

Carson-DeWitt, Rosalyn, ed. *Encyclopedia of Drugs,
   Alcohol, and Addictive Behavior.* 2nd ed. New York,
   NY: Macmillan Reference USA, 2001.

Drug Enforcement Agency. "Operation Running
   Waters Leads to Major PCP Arrests."
   September 4, 2003. Retrieved May 2013 (http://
   www.justice.gov/dea/pubs/states/newsrel/2003/
   la090403.html).

Drug Policy Alliance. "Drug War Statistics."
   Retrieved April 2013 (http://www.drugpolicy
   .org/drug-war-statistics).

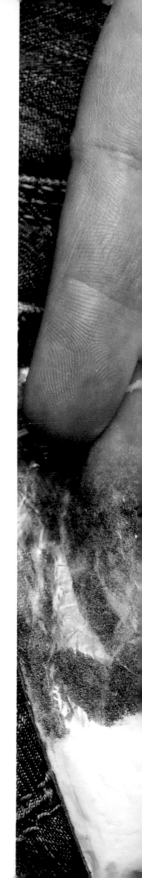

Fahrenthold, David A. "Use of PCP Rebounding in DC Area;
    Violence Follows Rise in Drug's Popularity." *Washington Post,*
    January 5, 2003. Retrieved May 2013 (http://www.highbeam
    .com/doc/1P2-239570.html).

Fundukian, Laurie J., and Jeffrey Wilson, eds. "Phencyclidine and
    Related Disorders." *Gale Encyclopedia of Mental Health.* Vol.
    2. 2nd ed. Detroit, MI: Gale, 2008.

Health Canada. "PCP (Phencyclidine)." Retrieved May 2013
    (http://www.hc-sc.gc.ca/hc-ps/drugs-drogues/learn
    -renseigne/pcp-eng.php#b).

Jares, Sue Ellen. "So Much for Cocaine and LSD—Angel Dust Is
    America's Most Dangerous New Drug." *People*, September
    4, 1978. Retrieved March 2013 (http://www.people.com/
    people/archive/article/0,,20071627,00.html).

KidsGrowth.com. "Teens Abusing Cold Remedies in Record
    Numbers to Attain PCP-like High" Retrieved March 2013
    (http://www.kidsgrowth.com/resources/articledetail
    .cfm?id=1766).

Korsmeyer, Pamela, and Henry R. Kranzler, eds. "Phencyclidine
    (PCP): Adverse Effects." *Encyclopedia of Drugs, Alcohol, and
    Addictive Behavior.* Vol. 3. 3rd ed. New York, NY: Macmillan
    Reference USA, 2009.

Loviglio, Joann. "All Wet, Dangerous New High: Kids Use
    Embalming Fluid as Recreational Drug." Associated Press,
    July 27, 2003. Retrieved May 2013 (http://www
    .theswitchboard.net/index.php?topic=6550.5;wap2).

Mumola, Christopher J., and Jennifer C. Karberg. *Drug Use and Dependence, State and Federal Prisoners, 2004.* Washington, DC: Bureau of Justice Statistics, 2006.

National Drug Intelligence Center. "Fry Fast Facts: Questions and Answers." November 2004. Retrieved May 2013 (http://www.justice.gov/archive/ndic/pubs11/12208/).

National Drug Intelligence Center. "PCP Fast Facts." May 2003. Retrieved May 2013 (http://www.justice.gov/archive/ndic/pubs4/4440/index.htm).

National Drug Intelligence Center. "PCP: Increasing Availability and Abuse." September 2004. Retrieved May 2013 (http://www.justice.gov/archive/ndic/pubs8/8180/8180p.pdf).

National Institute on Drug Abuse. "Trends and Statistics." Retrieved January 2013 (http://www.drugabuse.gov/related-topics/trends-statistics).

Substance Abuse and Mental Health Services Administration. "Drug Abuse Warning Network (DAWN)." 2013. Retrieved May 2013 (http://www.samhsa.gov/data/DAWN.aspx).

INDEX

About the Author

Christine Poolos writes and edits books and articles for young adults. She earned a BA from Colby College and an MA in writing from New York University.

Photo Credits

Cover, pp. 1, 10 U.S. DEA; p. 5 Christa Brunt/E+/Getty Images; pp. 7, 15, 24, 34, 44, 52, 54, 58, 59, 62 Sinisa Botas/Shutterstock.com; p. 8 MSPhotographic/Shutterstock.com; p. 12 Robert Nickelsberg/ Getty Images; pp. 17, 18, 23 © AP Images; p. 20 Martin M. Rotker/ Photo Researchers/Getty Images; p. 26 Bloomberg/Getty Images; pp. 28, 39 Scott Olson/Getty Images; p. 30 © A. Ramey/PhotoEdit; p. 35 Julia Pivovarova/E+/Getty Images; p. 42 Michaela Begsteiger/ Getty Images; p. 46 John Sommer/E+/Getty Images; p. 48 sturti/E+/ Getty Images; p. 50 Richard Clark/E+/Getty Images.

Designer: Sam Zavieh; Photo Researcher: Marty Levick